S0-AJX-893

Palo Alto City Library

The individual borrower is responsible for all library material borrowed on his or her card.

Charges as determined by the CITY OF PALO ALTO will be assessed for each overdue item.

Damaged or non-returned property will be billed to the individual borrower by the CITY OF PALO ALTO.

P.O. Box 10250, Palo Alto, CA 94303

The Snowflake

The SNOWFLAKE
A Water Cycle Story

NEIL WALDMAN

The Millbrook Press
Brookfield, Connecticut

Copyright © 2003 by Neil Waldman
All rights reserved

Library of Congress Cataloging-in-Publication Data
Waldman, Neil.
The snowflake : a water cycle story / Neil Waldman.
p. cm.
Summary: Follows the journey of a water droplet through the various
stages of the water cycle, from precipitation to evaporation and
condensation.
ISBN 0-7613-2347-3 (trade) — ISBN 0-7613-1762-7 (lib. bdg.)
1. Hydrologic cycle—Juvenile literature. 2. Snowflakes—Juvenile
literature. [1. Hydrologic cycle.] I. Title.
GB848.W34 2003
551.48—dc21
2003004806

Published by The Millbrook Press, Inc.
2 Old New Milford Road
Brookfield, Connecticut 06804
www.millbrookpress.com

Printed in the United States of America
5 4 3 2 1 (lib.)
5 4 3 2 1 (trade)

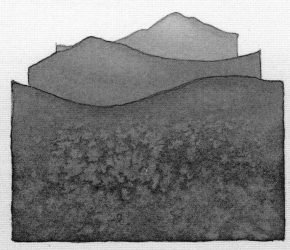

to Fred Dolan
and the kids of PS/MS 306

JANUARY

On a moonless night, a tiny snowflake
fell from a great gray cloud. It floated
slowly downward with thousands of
other flakes, coming to rest on the
jagged peak of a mountain.

FEBRUARY

A wind whistled over the mountain, carrying the snowflake back up into the air. The snowflake twisted and spun, swirling into a pond on the mountainside. The snowflake melted into a droplet, but as the days grew colder the pond froze.

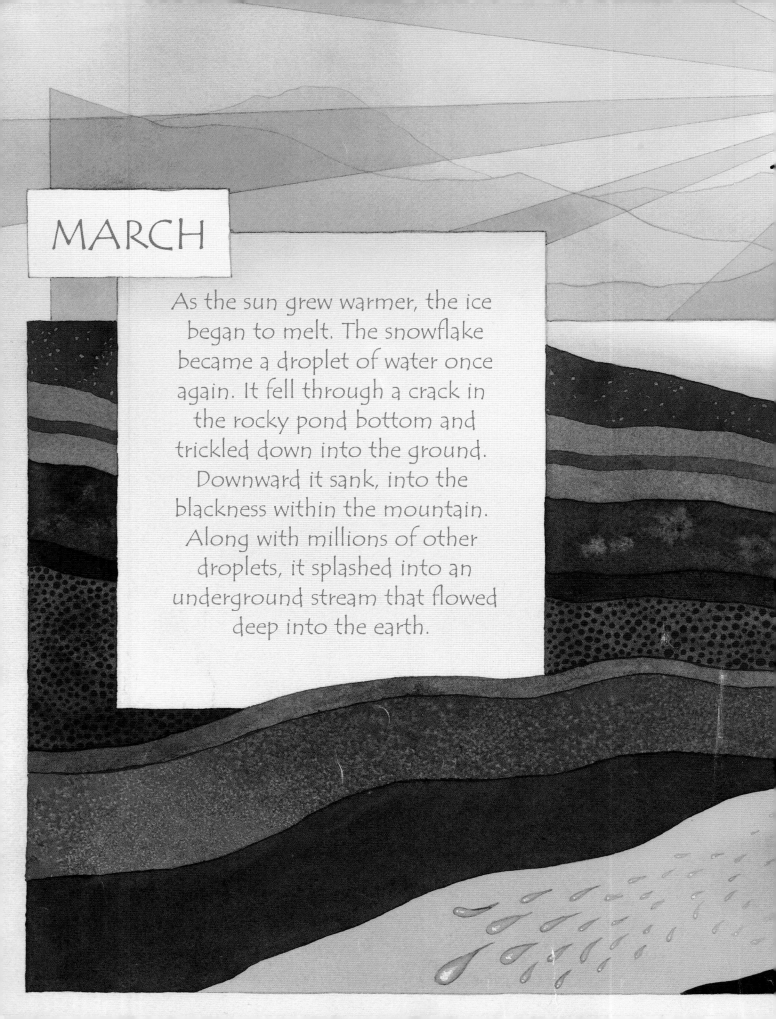

MARCH

As the sun grew warmer, the ice began to melt. The snowflake became a droplet of water once again. It fell through a crack in the rocky pond bottom and trickled down into the ground. Downward it sank, into the blackness within the mountain. Along with millions of other droplets, it splashed into an underground stream that flowed deep into the earth.

APRIL

After a long journey, the stream turned upward, bubbling through the ground in an icy spring. Sparkling in the sunlight, the droplet rushed into a brook. It danced around some stones, spilled over a waterfall, and surged into a raging river. The droplet flowed past villages and cities, under a great gray bridge where cars and buses carried people to and fro.

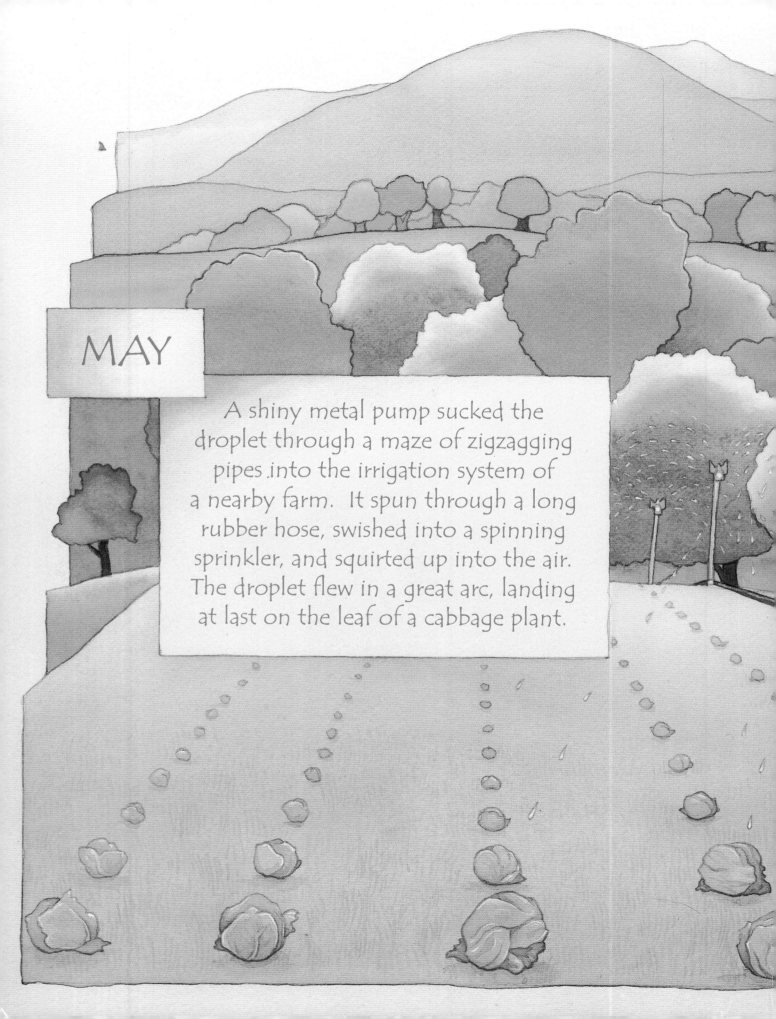

MAY

A shiny metal pump sucked the droplet through a maze of zigzagging pipes into the irrigation system of a nearby farm. It spun through a long rubber hose, swished into a spinning sprinkler, and squirted up into the air. The droplet flew in a great arc, landing at last on the leaf of a cabbage plant.

JUNE

In the chill of morning, a heavy blanket of fog rolled in over the farm. The droplet slowly evaporated and floated up into the thick grayness. But soon the rising sun began to bake the air as the fog rose high into the sky and became a cloud.

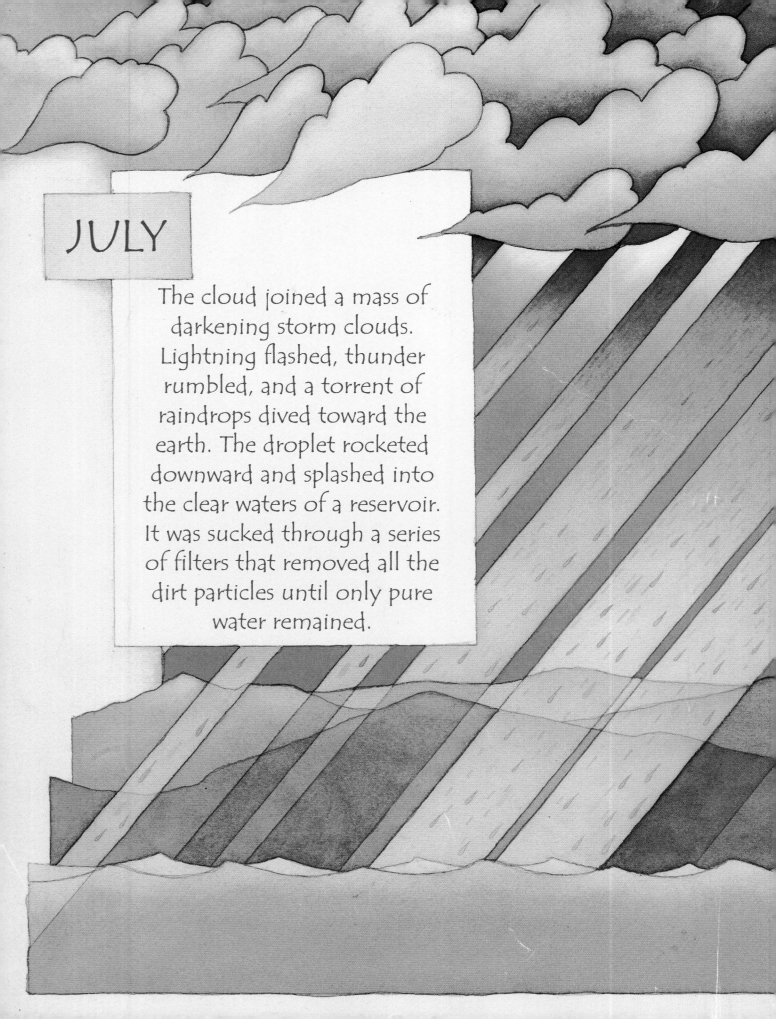

JULY

The cloud joined a mass of darkening storm clouds. Lightning flashed, thunder rumbled, and a torrent of raindrops dived toward the earth. The droplet rocketed downward and splashed into the clear waters of a reservoir. It was sucked through a series of filters that removed all the dirt particles until only pure water remained.

AUGUST

The droplet swished
through a long metal pipe.
It was pumped into a smaller pipe,
and then into an even smaller pipe,
where it suddenly stopped
and started
and stopped
and started again
in herky-jerky motions.

SEPTEMBER

In her bathroom, a young girl
twisted a faucet, and the droplet
poured out into a bathroom sink.
The girl dipped her hands into the
water and lifted the droplet onto
her cheek. A second later it was
falling, falling, falling,
splashing, swishing, spinning
through the drain
into another dark pipe.

OCTOBER

After a long, dark journey,
the droplet poured out into
the ocean. It flowed past
fields of waving sea grasses,
over corals of many colors,
and into the mouth of
a great striped fish.
Passing through the fish's
body, the droplet returned
to the sea.

NOVEMBER

Rising up to the ocean's surface,
the droplet was pulled steadily
toward the shore. On the
crest of a mighty wave, it
bubbled into foam, crashing
onto the sandy beach
of a tropical island.

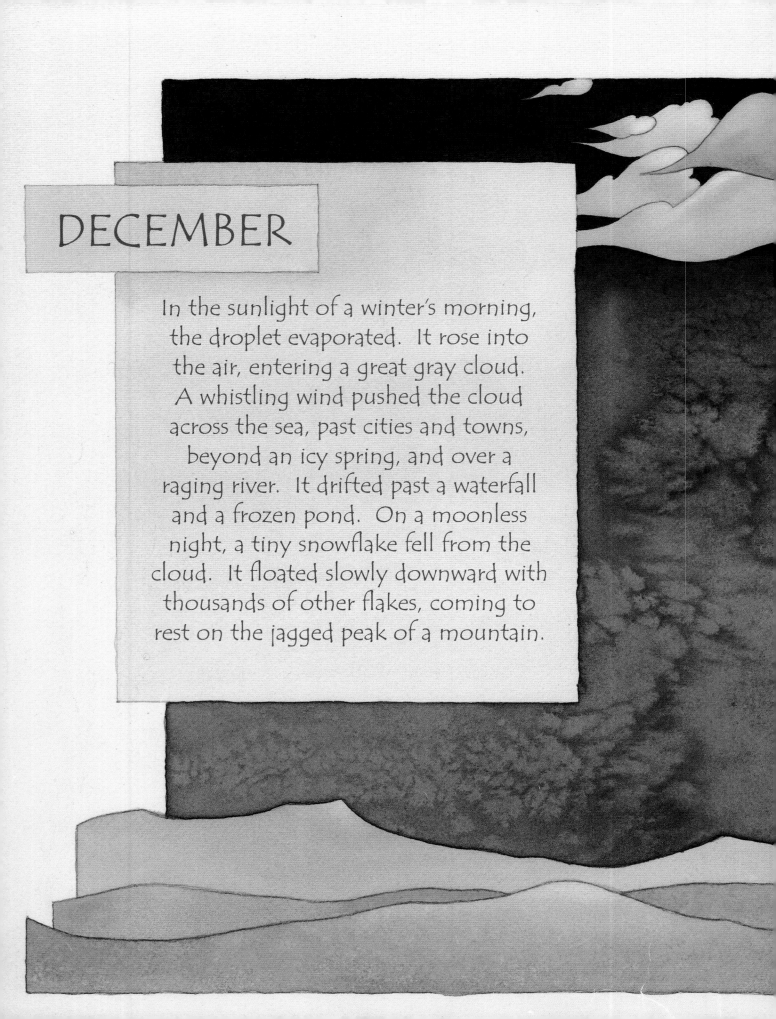

DECEMBER

In the sunlight of a winter's morning, the droplet evaporated. It rose into the air, entering a great gray cloud. A whistling wind pushed the cloud across the sea, past cities and towns, beyond an icy spring, and over a raging river. It drifted past a waterfall and a frozen pond. On a moonless night, a tiny snowflake fell from the cloud. It floated slowly downward with thousands of other flakes, coming to rest on the jagged peak of a mountain.

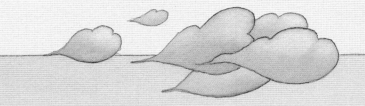

For years and years,
water has been freezing,
melting, evaporating, condensing,
and freezing again.
It travels all over the world,
and in its many forms, water has been
around far longer than people have.
In fact, water has been here almost
as long as the Earth itself.
So the next time you throw a snowball,
or jump into a swimming pool,
or drink some ice water
on a hot summer's day,
stop and think for a moment…

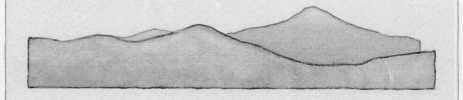

because some of that very
water might have tumbled
over Niagara Falls,
or risen as morning mist
in the steaming jungles of Africa,
or lay frozen for centuries
inside a glacier
on the North Pole.
It might have been sipped
by your great-grandmother
in a cup of afternoon tea.
It might have been used
by Abraham Lincoln
to scrub his hands
before dinner in the White House.
It might even have been guzzled
by a thirsty Tyrannosaurus rex
in a prehistoric swamp
millions of years ago.